Doves

G E O R G E K. P E C K

SMART APPLE MEDIA

Published by

Smart Apple Media

123 South Broad Street

Mankato, Minnesota 56001

☗

Copyright © 1998 Smart Apple Media.

Photos by George K. Peck,

Mark Peck,

Bob Thornburg Photography, Sid & Shirley Rucker / GeoImagery,

Sunstock / UNIPHOTO

Editorial assistance by Barbara Ciletti

Library of Congress Cataloging-in-Publication Data

Peck, George K.

Doves / written by George Peck.

p. cm.

Includes index.

Summary: Describes physical characteristics, habitats, and habits of some of

the numerous species of doves and pigeons.

ISBN 1-887068-16-3

1. Columbidae—Juvenile literature.   [1. Pigeons.]   I. Title.

QL696.C63P435   1998   96-18155

598.6'5—dc20   CIP

AC

First Edition   5 4 3 2 1

C O N T E N T S

or thousands

of years the dove

has symbolized

hope and peace.

In the Bible story of Noah's Ark, the earth was covered by a great flood. Only Noah and the animals on his ark survived. The ark came to rest atop a mountain. Noah sent forth a dove to search for dry land. When the dove returned, Noah knew that it was safe to leave the ark.

For the dove carried a green olive branch in its bill.

The dove described in the story of Noah could have been the bird we now call the Rock Dove, also known as the Common Pigeon. It is one of our oldest domesticated animals. More than 4,000 years ago, Rock Doves were raised in Egypt for food. They were also used to carry important messages long distances. Julius Caesar used them to send news of his victories back to Rome. Until the invention of the telegraph, domesticated Rock Doves were the fastest way to communicate over long distances!

There are more than 300 species of wild doves and pigeons in the Columbidae family. The larger members of the family are usually called pigeons and the smaller species are commonly called doves, but there is no scientific distinction between them. Sometimes the two words are used for the same bird, as in the case of the Rock Dove, better known as the Common Pigeon.

Doves and pigeons live all over the world, except in the colder polar regions. They are common in the biggest cities, in open deserts, and in dense forests. Some species live mostly in trees, while others spend most of their time on the ground. They may be sociable birds, living in groups, or solitary. Some, such as the Mourning Dove, are sociable during part of the year and solitary at other times.

Eight native dove and pigeon species now live and breed in the United States and Canada. Four other species—the Rock Dove, the Eurasian Collared-Dove, the Ringed Turtle Dove, and the Spotted Dove—were originally brought to North America by settlers and now live and breed in the wild. The Rock Dove is one of the best known birds of our cities and towns. The other non-native species also live near people, where food is plentiful and they can nest on buildings and other man-made structures.

Our best known native dove, the Mourning Dove, is found in a wide variety of habitats throughout southern Canada and the continental United States. The White-winged Dove lives in the desert regions of the southwestern

United States. The Band-tailed Pigeon can be found in oak and pine forests in the West.

The Passenger Pigeon, a native species that was once the most numerous bird in North America, is now extinct. Passenger Pigeons once lived throughout the deciduous forests of eastern North America, feeding on acorns, beechnuts, and chestnuts. In the 1800s, most of the eastern forests were cleared to farm the land. Loss of habitat and overhunting eventually caused the Passenger Pigeons to die off.

Doves vary greatly in size. Australia's Diamond Dove is only 7 1/2 inches (19 cm) in length, including its long tail. The Plain-breasted Ground-Dove of Central America has a slightly larger body, but because it has a short tail, it is less than 6 inches (15.3 cm) long. Both of these tiny doves are about the size of the common House Sparrow.

The largest living dove is the Blue-crowned Pigeon of New Guinea. It measures 33 inches (84 cm) long, about the size of a small turkey.

An early relative of the dove family, the flightless Dodo, once lived on the island of Mauritius in the Indian Ocean. An adult Dodo weighed as much as 50 pounds (23 kg)! Dodos have been extinct since 1681.

Most doves have small heads, plump bodies, and thick, fleshy legs. Their feet have short, curved claws and are adapted for both walking and perching. Legs and feet are usually pink or reddish. They have straight bills, slightly downturned at the tip, with a fleshy area at the base called a cere. Bills can be yellow, pink, red, black, or a combination of these colors.

Ground-dwelling doves have short, rounded wings. Other species have longer, pointed wings. The Mourning Dove has a long, pointed tail. The Common Ground-Dove's tail is short and fan-shaped.

Domestic pigeon varieties, descended from the wild Rock Dove, may have very different body shapes. The White King is raised, like chickens and turkeys, for food. It is a short, stocky, broad-breasted bird with pure white plumage. The "pouter" pigeon has long legs and a puffed-out chest. The "fantail" pigeon has a large, fan-shaped tail, and the "fairy swallow" has feet covered by long feathers.

Doves and pigeons have soft, thick feathers that easily pull out of the skin. The most common colors are pale shades of brown, gray, and pink, but some species, such as the Pink-necked Green-Pigeon of New Guinea, are among the most colorful of birds.

Males and females of most species are difficult to tell apart. The male and female Mourning Dove look nearly identical with grayish-brown backs and wings and a pinkish wash on their undersides. The Spotted Dove has a distinctive white-spotted black collar around the back of its neck. The White-winged Dove, a native southwestern species, looks a lot like the Mourning Dove, but it has white bands on its wings and a shorter, rounded tail.

Ground doves are some of our best camouflaged birds. When they are feeding or nesting on the ground, their mottled gray and brown feathers make them almost invisible.

Some of the most beautiful and unusual colorations are found on the common pigeons that inhabit our parks and city streets. If you look at a typical group of city pigeons you will see an amazing variety of colors, from pure white to shades of brown, rust, pink, green, and gold.

Common city pigeons are descended from the wild Rock Dove. The Rock Dove, the ancestor of all domestic pigeons, has slate gray plumage, a white rump, two black bars on the wings, a black band on the tip of the tail, and iridescent green and purple feathers on the neck.

D O V E S

A Rock Dove in Ontario.

Ground-feeding doves eat a variety of seeds and grains. Some doves also eat grasses, leaves, insects, and snails. The Band-tailed Pigeon feeds on fruits and berries. In the Southwest, the White-winged Dove eats cactus fruit in addition to seeds and grains.

Doves will eat many different foods, depending on what is available. In the wild, the Rock Dove feeds mostly on seeds and grains. But Rock Doves that live in our cities are happy eating bits of bread, popcorn, and cookies.

When hard seeds and grains are part of their diet, doves will also swallow small bits of gravel and sand. This grit is stored in a muscular part of the stomach called the gizzard. The grit helps the gizzard grind up the hard seeds, making them easier to digest.

Have you ever watched a bird drink? Most birds drink by dipping their bills into the water, getting a mouthful, then raising their heads to swallow. They do this again and again until they aren't thirsty anymore. Doves drink differently from other birds. They dip their bills in just once and suck up water until their thirst is satisfied.

A White-tipped Dove feeding in Texas.

Most doves are strong flyers, but the champion of the family is the Homing Pigeon, a domesticated breed of Rock Dove. One of the swiftest of all birds, the "homer" can fly 82 miles per hour (132 kph). The Homing Pigeon was originally bred to carry messages home. Wherever it is released, it has the amazing ability to find its way back to its home loft. In the sport of pigeon racing, "homers" are taken many miles from their home loft and released to see how fast they can find their way back.

One pigeon owned by the Duke of Wellington was released in southwest Africa and found its way back to England, 5,700 miles (9,170 km) away. Unfortunately for the bird, it was found dead just one mile from its home loft.

Passenger Pigeons were also swift flyers—estimated to reach speeds of 70 miles per hour (112 kph)—but not swift enough to escape the shotguns of hunters. The Mourning Dove can fly at speeds of 55 miles per hour (88 kph). Even the Common Ground-Dove, with its short wings and small body, can reach speeds of 32 miles per hour (51 kph).

If doves are startled or take flight suddenly, they will sometimes clap their wings together over their backs. Wing clapping is also performed by male doves during courtship.

In the fall, some North American dove species migrate south in search of warmer weather and more plentiful food. The Mourning Dove may travel only a few hundred miles. The western Band-tailed Pigeon migrates from

British Columbia, Washington, and Oregon down into California and Mexico.

The Rock Dove, an urban dweller, does not migrate at all, even though it is capable of flying long distances quickly. Southern species such as the Common Ground-Dove and the Inca Dove also stay in the same areas.

C O U R T S H I P

If you live in a city, you have probably heard the *coo-a-roo* of the Rock Dove, or Common Pigeon. The sad-sounding *coah, cooo, cooo, coo* of the Mourning Dove is often heard in our backyards and gardens. Other dove species have their distinctive "coos" too.

The doves' cooing is most often heard in the spring when the male dove coos to attract female doves and to warn other males away from his territory. The courting male will also "show off" to the female by bowing, spreading his tail, bobbing his head, and strutting. Rock Doves will often turn in complete circles, performing a kind of dance for the female. Courtship might also include repeated wing clapping while in flight, and the males often peck at the females at the beginning of their courtship. Fights between males can be ferocious.

A more gentle part of courtship is called "billing." The male opens his bill and the female puts her bill into his mouth. In some species, the male feeds the female.

After courtship, the pair mate and a nest site is selected, usually by the male. The area near the nest is defended by both the male and the female. Some dove species, such as the Mourning Dove, usually nest alone. Others nest in colonies. The Passenger Pigeon nested in huge colonies. One Passenger Pigeon colony in Wisconsin covered 850 square miles (2210 km²) of forest and contained 136 million birds!

Doves nest in a variety of places. The wild Rock Dove nests in caves or crevices on cliffs. Its city relatives nest on ledges, beams, rafters, and other parts of buildings and bridges. The Common Ground-Dove often nests on the ground. Some dove species nest in tree cavities or use the abandoned nests of other birds. The Mourning Dove builds a twiggy nest in trees or shrubs. In desert areas, they will even nest in prickly cactus plants or on the ground.

Once the nest site has been chosen and the nest built, the female lays one or two eggs. The eggs are usually pure white, though some doves lay cream- or coffee-colored eggs.

Rock Doves may nest at any time of the year, raising several broods of young doves. Mourning Doves nest from March through October and can raise up to three broods a year.

The eggs must stay warm to help the baby doves inside them grow. Both the male and female doves take turns sitting on the eggs. The male usually sits on the eggs during the day, the female at night. Before the eggs are laid, the adult birds get a brood patch, or a bare patch of warm skin on their bellies. The heat from the warm patch of skin helps the baby doves grow quickly. The eggs hatch in 14 to 15 days.

The eggs and nest of a White-winged Dove in Texas.

While they are still inside their eggs, baby doves grow a hard bump called an egg tooth on their bills. Most baby birds have an egg tooth. Without it, they wouldn't be able to break out of their shells.

Inside the egg, the baby dove pecks a circle at the large end of the shell, breaking it open. After the baby dove has hatched, the egg tooth falls off.

Doves are born helpless, with their eyes closed and only a slight covering of soft down. For the first few days, the baby doves are fed pigeon's milk, a thick, nutritious liquid made in their parents' crops. The crop is a pouch inside the bird's neck where food is stored. Both parents feed the babies, bringing pigeon's milk up from their crops into their mouths. The babies take the food right out of the parent's mouth.

As the babies grow older, the parents will add small insects and seeds to the babies' diet. They will continue to give the babies pigeon's milk until they are able to fly.

In a few days, stiff quills grow to replace the down. Feathers soon sprout from the quills. Within two weeks, the young birds are fully feathered and ready to fly. In another week, they will be on their own.

The male Mourning Dove feeding its nestlings.

Like all wild animals, doves face many dangers. About 70 percent of young doves will die in their first year. Eggs and nestlings can be destroyed by high winds. Many adult doves are killed by flying into TV antennas and utility wires.

Predators are a constant threat. Squirrels, raccoons, and snakes will raid nests and eat both eggs and young doves. Doves are a favorite food source for hawks and falcons.

The Peregrine Falcon, one of the world's swiftest birds, hunts doves every chance it gets. Peregrine Falcons now live in many cities, nesting on tall buildings and hunting for Rock Doves. When chased by a falcon, the Rock Dove will swoop around and between buildings and trees at tremendous speeds, swerving down and sideways and diving, in full flight, into any hole it sees.

In captivity a Mourning Dove can live as long as 17 years. Domesticated pigeons might live for 6 to 16 years. In the wild, it is possible for a Mourning Dove to live 10 years or longer, but few survive that long.

The dove's greatest enemy is the human hunter. In the 1800s, Passenger Pigeons were hunted to extinction. Fortunately, dove hunting is now regulated.

Hunting and loss of habitat, however, do threaten many other dove species. The Puerto Rican Plain Pigeon, the Mauritius Pink Pigeon, the Seychelles Turtle-Dove, and the Victoria Crowned-Pigeon of New Guinea are now endangered. Some species are extremely rare and are on the verge of extinction.

Doves and humans have had a close relationship for thousands of years. The Rock Dove, our oldest domesticated species, is still used for food, for the sport of pigeon racing, and for show. Rock Doves and Mourning Doves have adapted to humans and are some of the most common wild animals living in our towns and cities, but other species have suffered from human contact.

The extinction of the Passenger Pigeon is one of the most tragic examples of how humans can destroy a species. Two hundred years ago there were between three and five billion Passenger Pigeons in North America—more than a quarter of all the birds on the continent! In less than 100 years, overhunting and land clearing reduced their numbers to a few million, and then a few thousand. The last wild Passenger Pigeon was shot in Ohio in 1900. The last Passenger Pigeon on our planet died in a Cincinnati zoo on September 1, 1914.

I N D E X